BABIES OF AFRICA

Cubs, Calves, and Colts

AUTHOR/EDITOR: Emma Hammack
PHOTOGRAPHER: Paula Hammack

Copyright 2020

THE STERLING AFRICA FOUNDATION

Hammack.Ink

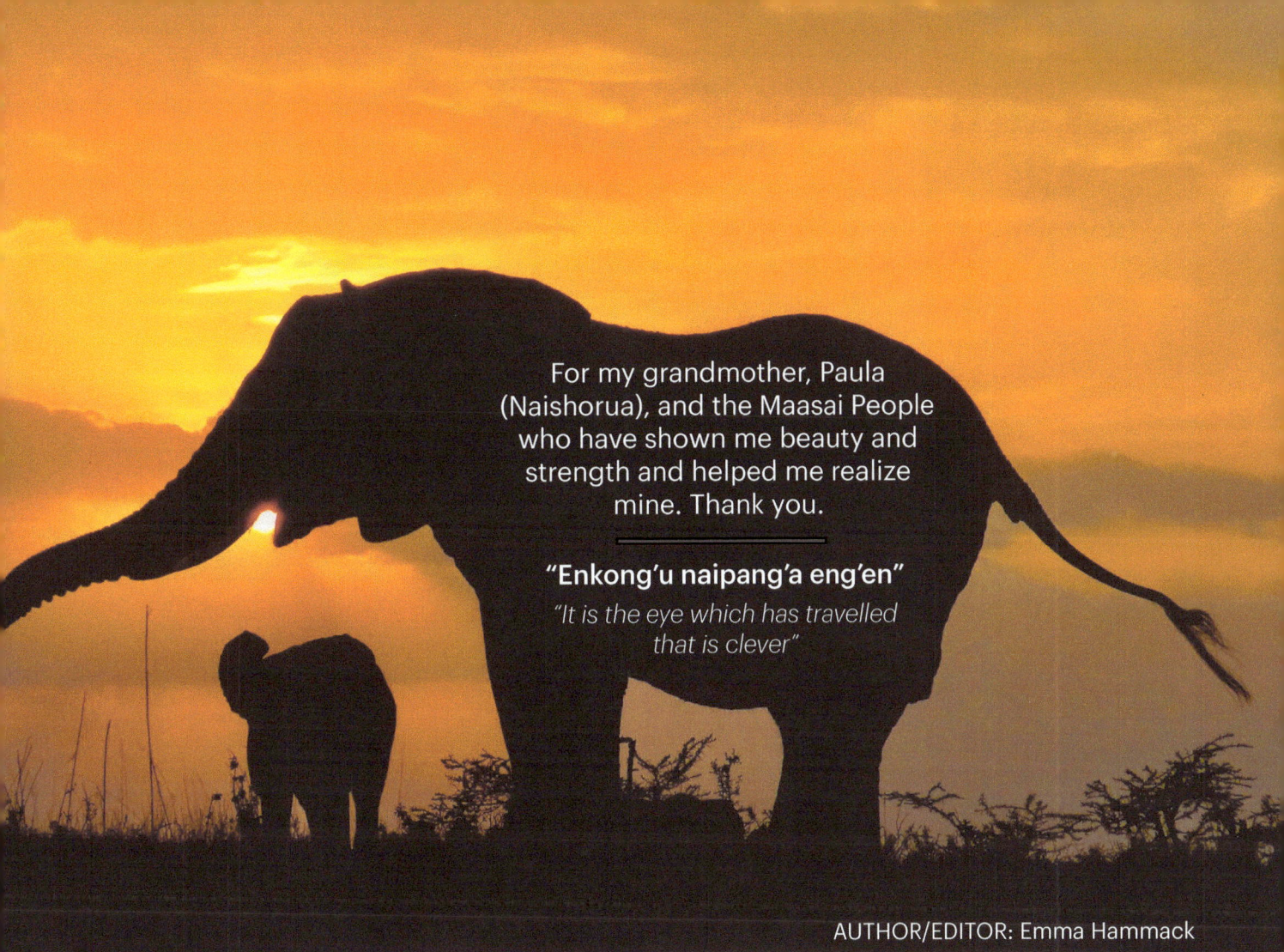

For my grandmother, Paula (Naishorua), and the Maasai People who have shown me beauty and strength and helped me realize mine. Thank you.

"Enkong'u naipang'a eng'en"

"It is the eye which has travelled that is clever"

AUTHOR/EDITOR: Emma Hammack

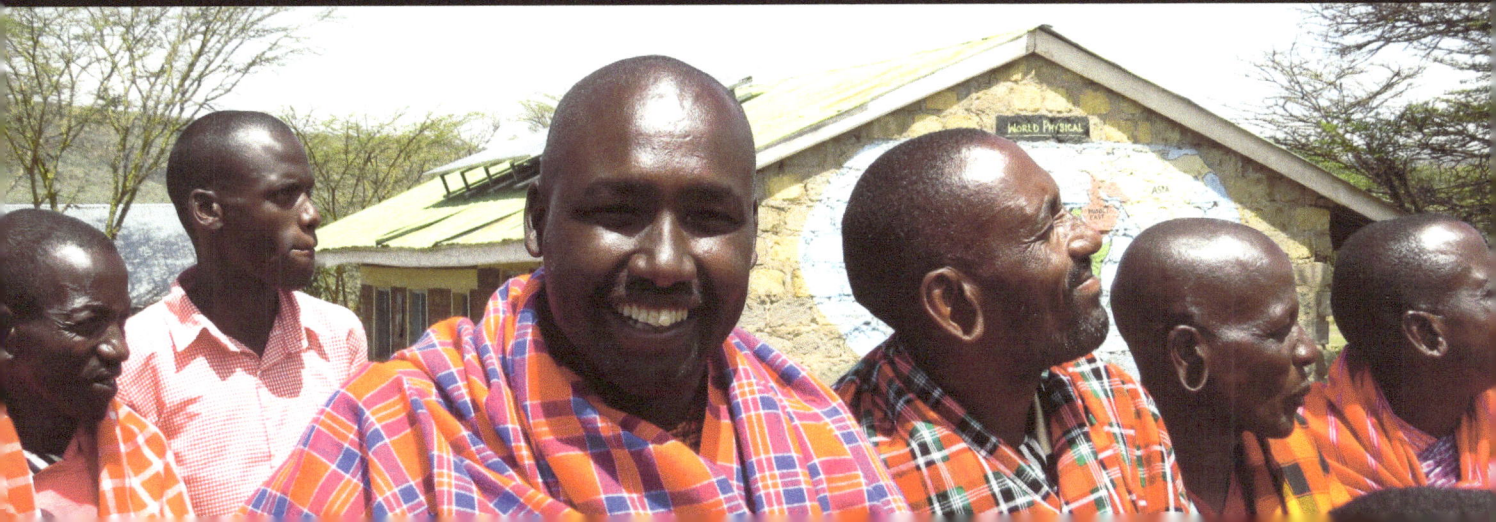

MOTHER AND CHILD BONDING

Baboon Mother looking down at her young baby who would like to be picked up.

Momma lioness leading her three cubs back to the den.

Mother hyena walking behind her playful, running cub.

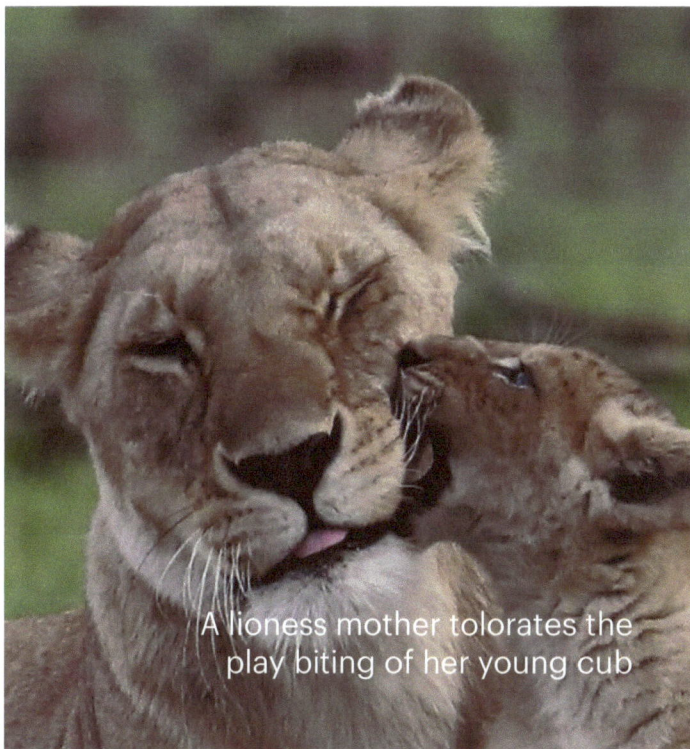

A lioness mother tolorates the play biting of her young cub

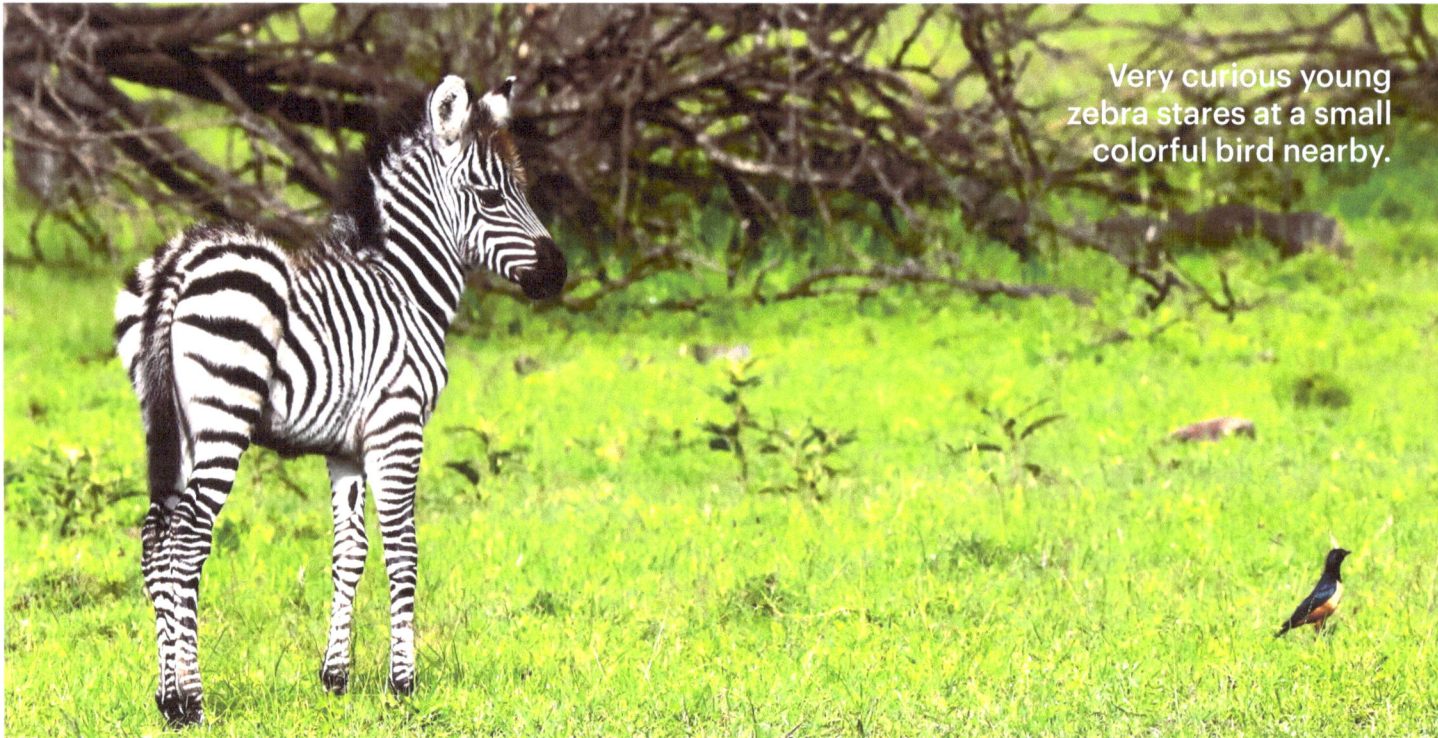

Very curious young zebra stares at a small colorful bird nearby.

Playful, curious young cheetah picks up feces and carries it in its mouth as it follows its mother.

YOUNG GIRAFFE AND IMPALA

BIG AND SMALL ANIMALS CAN BE SEEN TOGETHER IN THE MAASAI MARA

A young giraffe stops at a watering hole that appears to be empty, with its foot in the watering hole it turns its head away from the impala standing on the other side.

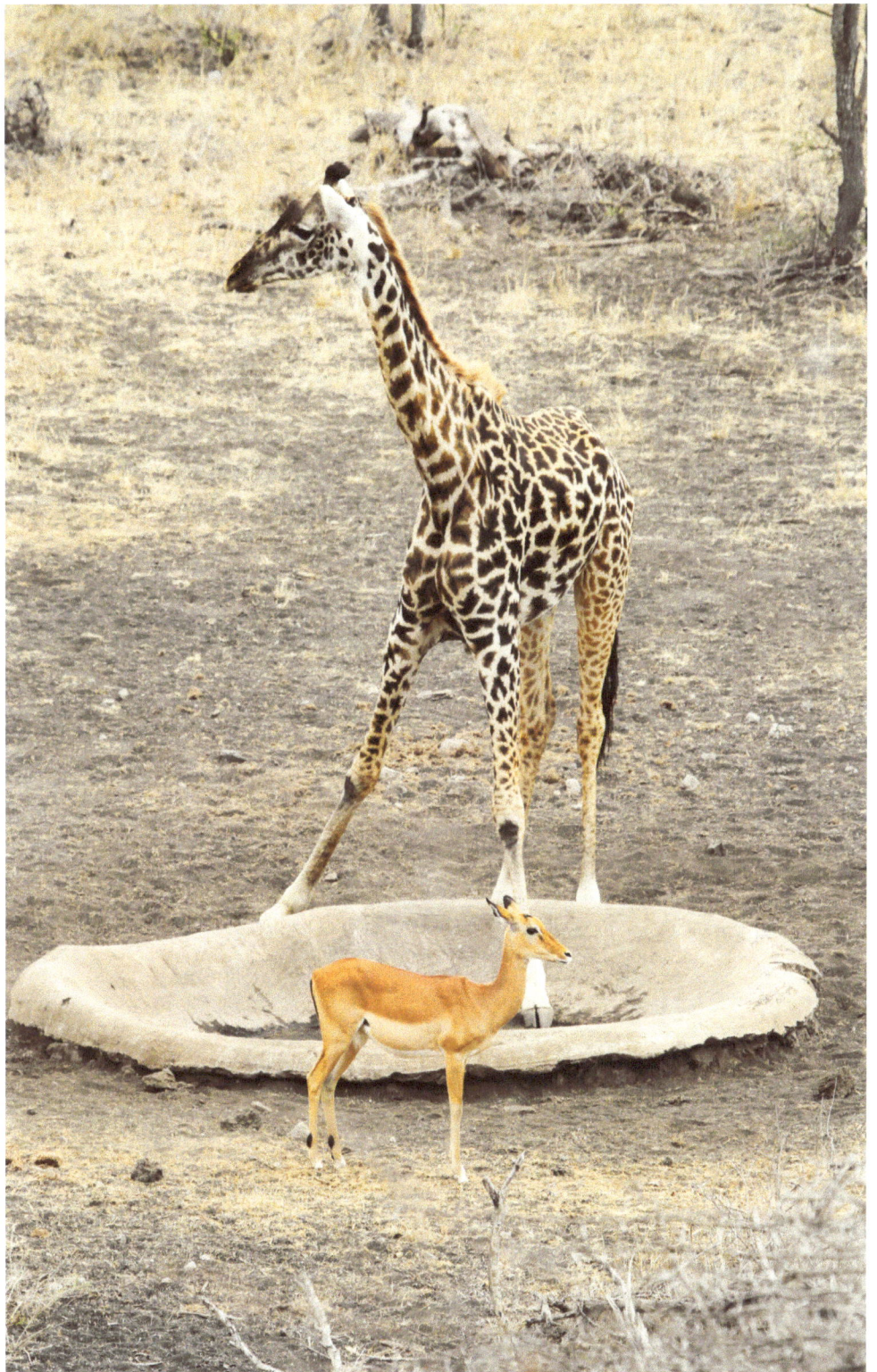

YOUTH IN THE FIELDS OF THE MAASAI MARA

HYENAS, BABOONS, AND LEOPARDS

Baby baboon catches a ride on its mom's back while strolling through the

Three hyena cubs playfully fight together.

Leopard mother calls her cubs to follow her while she hunts in the late

AFRICAN BUSH ELEPHANT AND CALF

THE PROTECTOR

Momma elephant keeps her young energetic calf close and keeps an eye out for any predators that are interested in her child, such as lions and hyenas.

CUBS AND CALVES

CHEETAHS, LIONS, ELEPHANTS AND ZEBRAS

Two lion cubs stay close to the lionesses in their den that is hidden well.

Two cheetah cubs playing look back at their mother.

A small zebra calf runs quickly through the green grass to its mother.

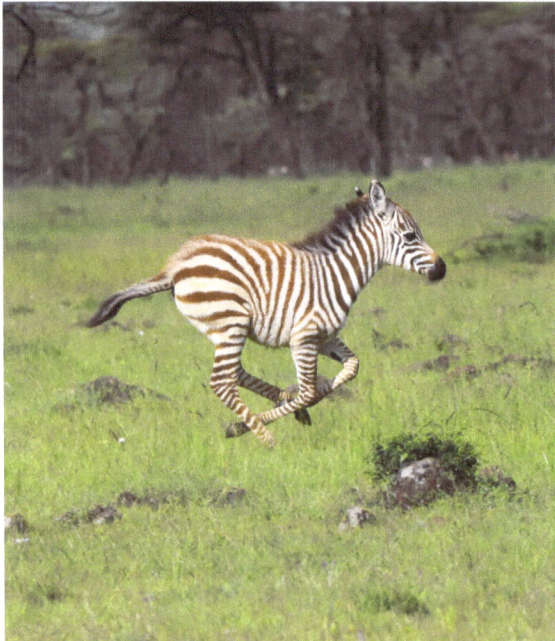

An elephant calf enjoys eating some yummy grass.

Lioness Mother and Her Four Cubs

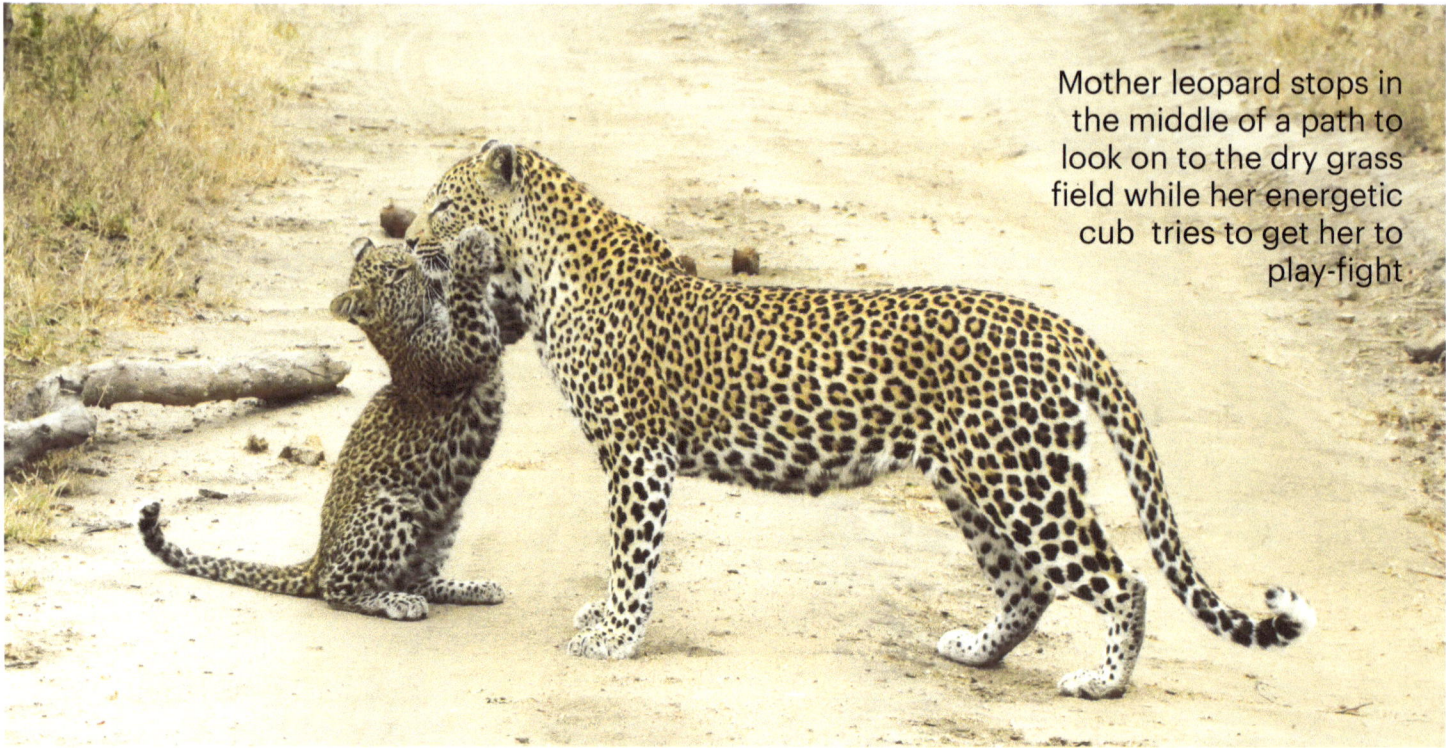

Mother leopard stops in the middle of a path to look on to the dry grass field while her energetic cub tries to get her to play-fight

A fluffy lion cub runs through the grass to its siblings

MOMS ALWAYS KEEP A CLOSE EYE

GIRAFFES, ZEBRAS AND OSTRICHES

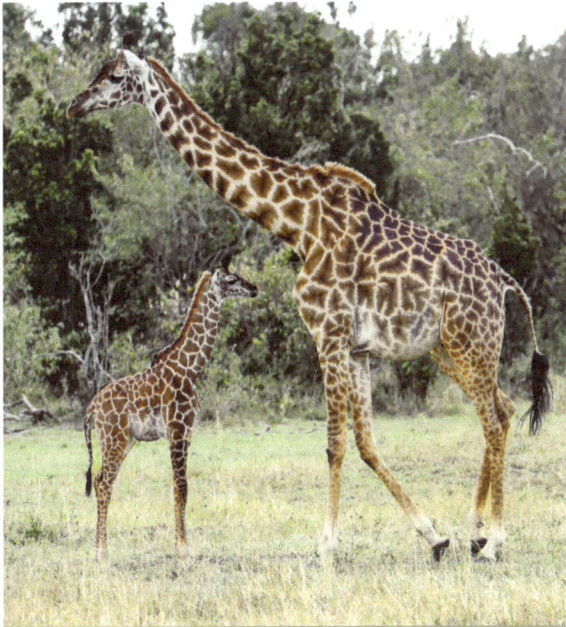

Momma giraffe walks towards her young calf who is already about 7 feet tall.

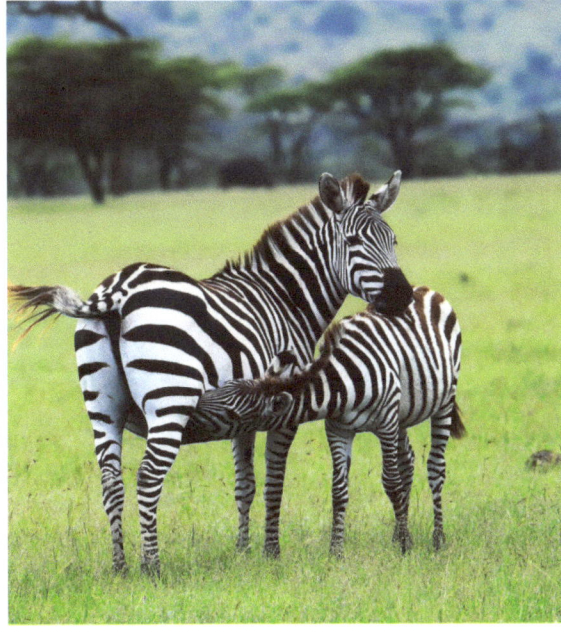

Mother zebra feeds her calf in the middle of field while watching her surroundings.

Ostrich mom walks slowly keeping her small chicks close together.

Female Cheetah named Fig keeps her young child close because she lost her other cub to predators.

MOTHER AND CHILD

ZEBRAS, TOPS, LIONS, AND ELEPHANTS

Playful zebra calf jumps overs its mother who is resting on the ground.

A topi and its calf look onto the open field in front of them.

A lioness carries its cub from the river to its den.

A mother elephant watches as her calf dances in front of her.

Two baby elephants use their trunks toplay with each other.

Two leopard cubs sitting on a tree.

PARENTING IN THE WILD

LIONS, BABOONS, ELEPHANTS AND HYNENAS

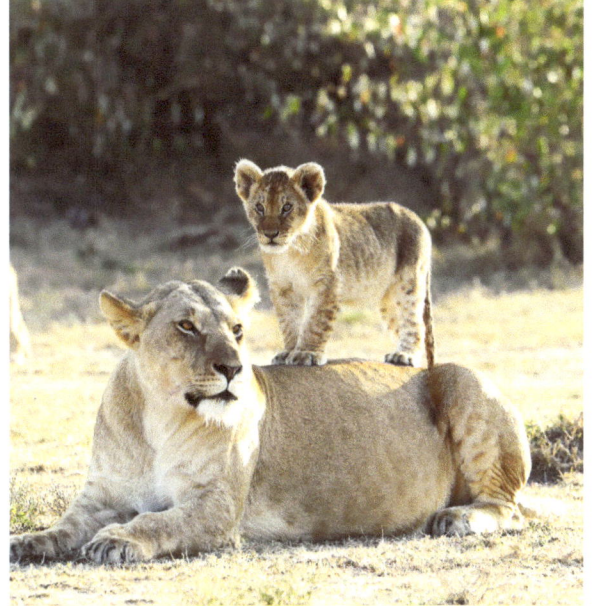
A baboon mommy nurses her baby.

A lion cub stands on its mother's back.

An elephant family having a fun time together.

Mother and rhino calf feeding on grass

Momma Hyena playing with her two babies

BABIES

ELEPHANT, IMPALA, LION AND DIK DIK

Elephant calf enjoys itself while eating grass.

Impala calf runs through the tall grass to its mother.

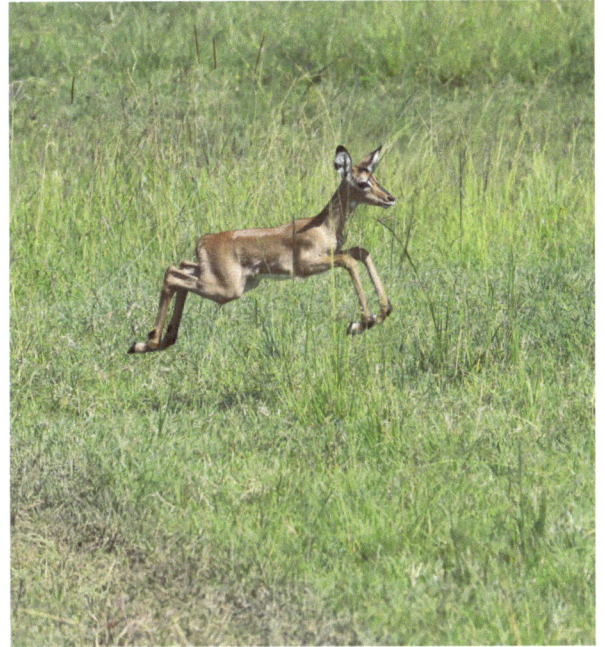

Playful lion cub jumps after the leaves on the tree.

A young dik dik stares intently at a stranger.

PLAYTIME

TWO CHEETAH CUBS

Two cheetah cubs play together. One climbs a tree, while the other lays in the shade. Cheetahs climb trees to watch their prey, rest, sleep, and they keep their prey up in trees once the catch it, so other predators don't steal it.

Two elephants stay close with the calf underneath them.

The mother lioness rests with her cubs in her paws and on her back.

Four lion cubs playing in a tree

TAKING CARE OF THE YOUNG

GIRAFFES, LIONS AND LEOPARDS

Three small giraffe calves walk in a line.

Mother lioness carries very young cub in her mouth.

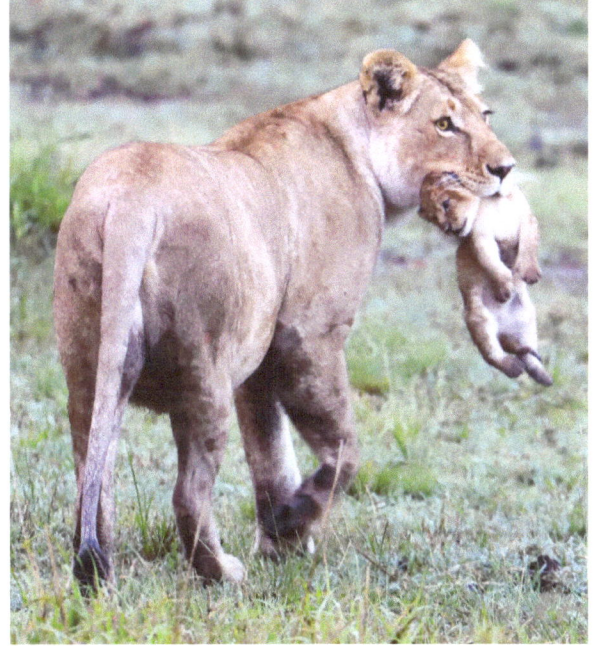

Momma leopard licks her older cub clean behind a bush.

White Rhino and calf grazing though dry grass.

Two baby monkeys try to get their mom to play with them.

UNCOMMON SIGHTING

WATERBUCKS

Here is a mother waterbuck and her calf in the tall grass and trees in the Maasai Mara. The waterbuck is part of the antelope family and eats grass and leaves from trees.

KEEPING THEM CLOSE

LIONS, WATERBUCKS AND LEOPARDS

Lioness carries her cub in her mouth back towards the den to put with the other cubs.

Mother waterbuck checks on her calf

Leopard momma cuddles with her older cub in the shade.

Mother hippo and her calf are out of the river eating grass.

Lioness comes back to her three cubs after a hunt to bring them all back to the den.

MOTHER KNOWS BEST
GIRAFFES, BABOONS, LEOPARDS AND ELEPHANTS

Three giraffes, with the youngest in the middle, huddle close to each other.

Momma baboon carries her baby on her back

Leopard mother brings her cub along side fo her to teach her baby how to hunt.

Elephant mom keeps her calf close under her.

Curious baby rhino and its mother feeding

CATS OF THE MAASAI MARA

LEOPARDS, LIONS AND CHEETAHS

Leopard mom brings along her two cubs to show them how to hunt.

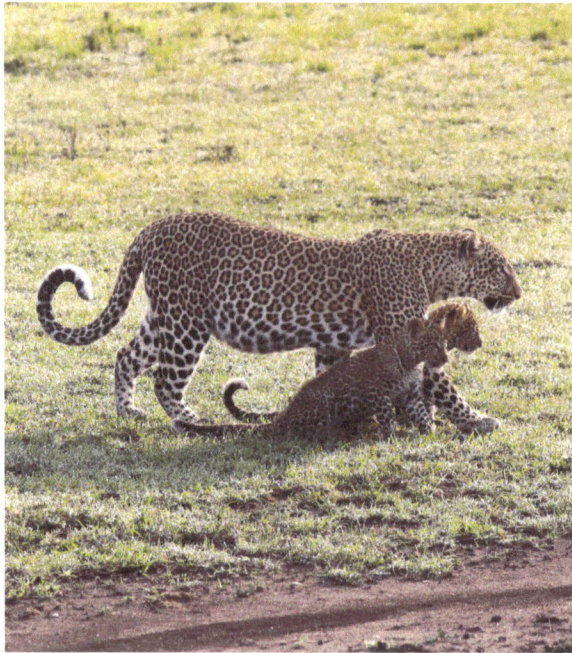

Mother Lioness mother tries to control her three cubs while resting underneath a bush.

Two cheetah cubs climbing up a tree at sunset.

LEARNING INDEPENDENCE
YOUNG LEOPARD

This young leopard on the prowl is learning how to hunt from its mother. Leopards usually leave their moms when they around 12-18 months old. .

CUBS OF ALL SIZES

LIONS AND LEOPARDS

Three small lion cubs wait in the grass for the lionesses to come back with food.

Two small leopard cubs sit in the grass.

Mother leopard and child rest by a bush.

Leopard and its cub stop in the middle of the path to look at field behind them with the cubs paws wrapped around its mom

Two lionesses and their six cubs

Two lion cubs play with a stick

Lion cub climbs
a big tree in the
Maasai Mara
Reserve while his
siblings watch him
struggle

STERLING AFRICA FOUNDATION

CREATING SELF-SUFFICIENCY FOR SUB-SAHARAN AFRICA

100% of the proceeds from this book will go directly to the Sterling Africa Foundation.

The Sterling Africa Foundation is a small foundation but they try to have a big impact on the small local Maasai and other disadvantaged communities in Kenya. These communities are underserved or ignored by the country's government and they struggle to meet the needs of their daily lives. The Sterling Africa Foundation helps dig wells, create water catchment systems, build schools, dormitories and a medical clinic, educate children and women, teach agriculture and alternative farming methods, and supports a medical clinic facility and staff.

Visit www.SterlingAfricaFoundation.org for more information on our charitable mission.

To buy pictures from this book and see our other spectacular pictures of animals and Africa, visit www.SAFphotos.com.

Sterling Africa Foundation, Inc.
A Charitible 501(c)(3) Organization
Tax ID# 45-3040059

Lifestraws which filter the water as you drink are a great help when clean water is a scarce.

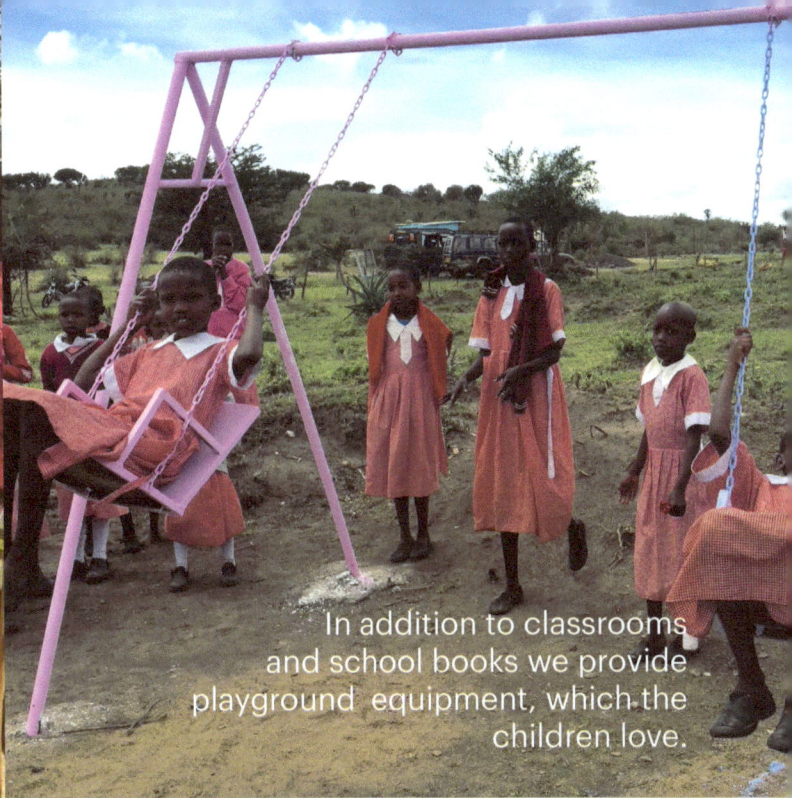
In addition to classrooms and school books we provide playground equipment, which the children love.

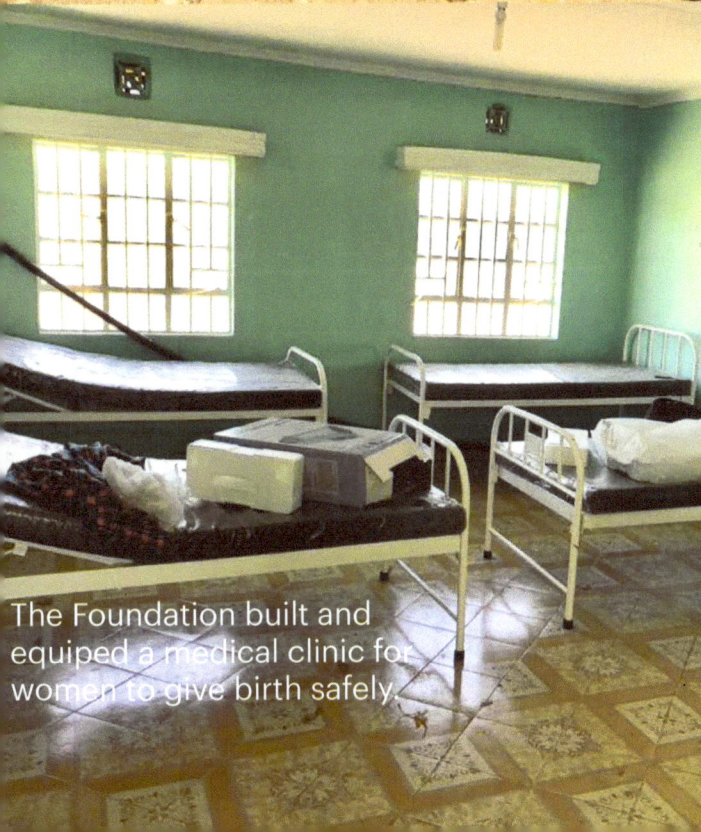
The Foundation built and equiped a medical clinic for women to give birth safely.

Water wells and catchments systems are crucial to the communities survival.

Thank you
for buying this book!

Your purchase will help buy
and grow food, purchase
school books for children,
build classrooms and water
catchment systems, dig
water wells and provide
for the medical needs for
disadvantaged communities in
Africa.

100% of the proceeds from this
book will go directly to the Sterling
Africa Foundation.

Visit www.SterlingAfricaFoundation.org for
more information on our charitable mission.
To buy pictures from this book and see our
other spectacular picturesof animals and
Africa, visit www.SAFphotos.com.

www.ingramcontent.com/pod-product-compliance
Lightning Source LLC
Chambersburg PA
CBHW060818270326
41930CB00002B/85